A+ books

3-D Shapes

Cones

by Nathan Olson

Capstone
press

Mankato, Minnesota

A+ Books are published by Capstone Press,
151 Good Counsel Drive, P.O. Box 669, Mankato, Minnesota 56002.
www.capstonepub.com

 Books published by Capstone Press are manufactured with paper
containing at least 10 percent post-consumer waste.

Library of Congress Cataloging-in-Publication Data
Olson, Nathan.
   Cones / by Nathan Olson.
      p. cm.—(A+ books. 3-D shapes)
   Summary: "Simple text and color photographs introduce cone shapes and give examples of cones
in the real world"—Provided by publisher.
   Includes bibliographical references and index.
   ISBN-13: 978-1-4296-0048-4 (hardcover)
   ISBN-10: 1-4296-0048-9 (hardcover)
   1. Cone—Juvenile literature. 2. Shapes—Juvenile literature. 3. Geometry, Solid—Juvenile literature.
I. Title. II. Series.
QA491.O44 2008
516'.154—dc22   2006037424

Credits
Jenny Marks, editor; Alison Thiele, designer; Scott Thoms and Charlene Deyle, photo researchers;
   Kelly Garvin, photo stylist

Photo Credits
Capstone Press/Alison Thiele, cover (illustration), 7 (illustration), 29 (illustrations); Karon Dubke, 4, 6,
   10, 11, 12–13, 23, 24–25, 29 (craft)
Corbis/Charles Gupton, 5; Charles Krebs, 21; Keren Su, 26
Courtesy of Thorsten Buchen, 27
The Image Works/Topham, 14–15
Index Stock Imagery/Glenn Kulbako, 8–9
iStockphoto/Egorych, 16–17
SeaPics.com/Marilyn & Maris Kazmers, 20
Shutterstock/Chen Wei Seng, 22; Magdalena Kucova, 19
SuperStock, Inc./Steve Vidler, 18

Note to Parents, Teachers, and Librarians
This 3-D Shapes book uses full color photographs and a nonfiction format to introduce the concept
of cone shapes. *Cones* is designed to be read aloud to a pre-reader or to be read independently
by an early reader. Photographs help listeners and early readers understand the text and concepts
discussed. The book encourages further learning by including the following sections: Table of
Contents, It's a Fact, Hands On, Glossary, Read More, Internet Sites, and Index. Early readers may
need assistance using these features.

Table of Contents

What Are 3–D Shapes? 4

Playing with Cones 8

Outdoor Cones 14

All Kinds of Cones 22

It's a Fact............................26

Hands On 28

Glossary 30

Read More 31

Internet Sites 31

Index 32

What Are 3-D Shapes?

Squares, triangles, and circles are two-dimensional shapes. These colorful magnets are all 2-D shapes.

Some shapes are not flat. They are 3-D, or three-dimensional. 3-D shapes have height, width, and depth.

Cones are 3-D shapes. The base of a cone is a circle and the top comes to a point.

base

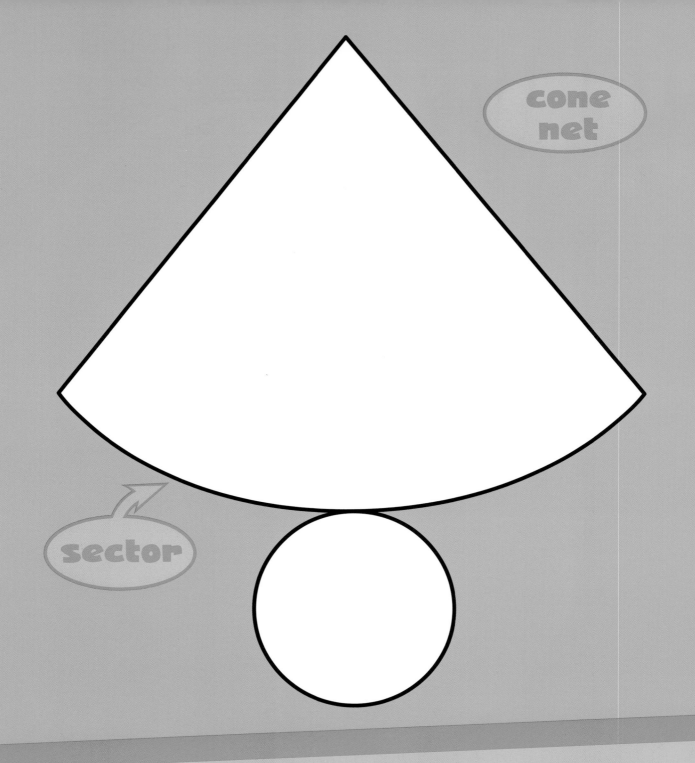

A cone is made of a circle and a part of another circle called a sector. These two flat shapes make the cone's net.

Playing with Cones

Cone–shaped megaphones make cheers sound louder.

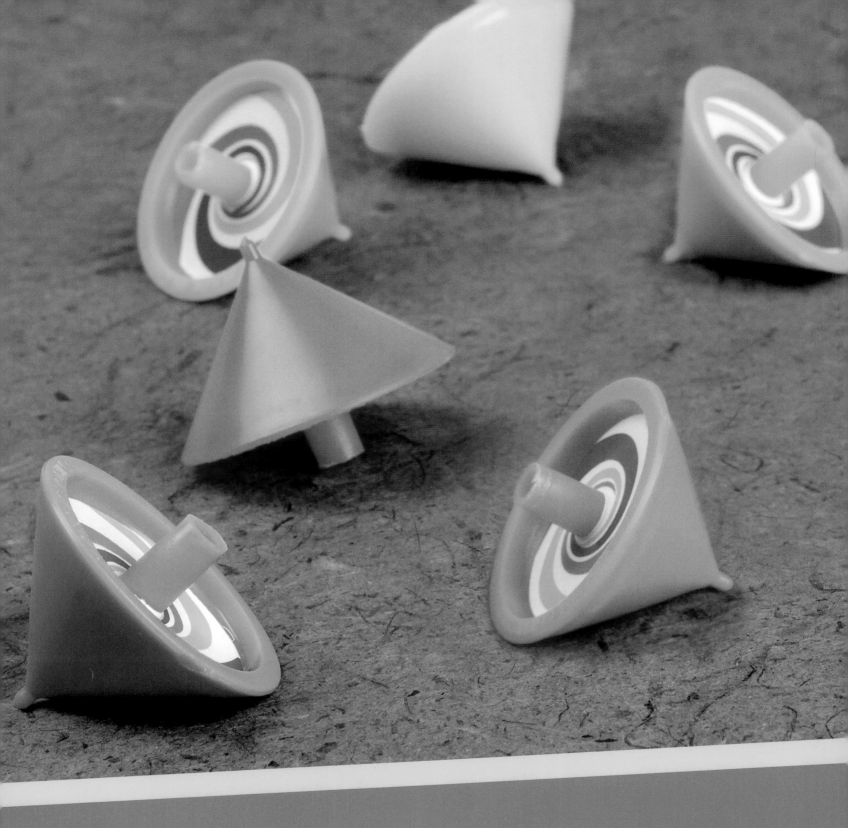

Tops are toy cones that
spin and whirl.

Pretend princesses wear
pretty cone hats.

Sand castles can be topped
with cone–shaped towers.

Outdoor Cones

Real castles have towers
with cone-shaped roofs.

Orange–and–white traffic cones guide drivers on the road.

CHERRY VALLEY DISTRICT LIBRARY

17

Volcanoes are nature's cones,
sometimes filled with fire and smoke.

Icicles sparkle like long,
thin cones in the wintry air.

19

Colorful cone–shaped shells
are homes for sea snails.

Little toadstools with cone–shaped tops pop up in the grass after a summer shower.

All Kinds of Cones

The powerful horn of a rhinoceros
is a giant nose cone.

What kind of picture can you draw with cone-shaped tips like these?

What's the tastiest cone of all?
The one holding your favorite
flavor of ice cream, of course!

It's a Fact

 The ice cream cone got its start at the 1904 World's Fair in St. Louis, Missouri. Two food sellers worked side by side. One sold ice cream in cups, and the other sold wafer cookies rolled into cylinders. One day the ice cream seller ran out of cups. The cookie seller rolled his wafers into cones instead of cylinders. The ice cream cone was born.

 Cone–shaped hats made of straw are popular in Vietnam, China, Korea, and Japan. People have worn this type of hat for hundreds of years as protection from the sun and rain.

The rhinoceros is one of the most endangered animals on the planet. Although it is against the law, people hunt rhinos for their horns. There are only five different kinds of rhinos alive today.

 Purple cone snails have long, sharp tongues filled with poison. When a fish comes close, the snail stings the fish with its tongue. The poisoned fish is unable to move, making it an easy meal for the snail.

 In Cologne, Germany, you'll find a 40-foot (12-meter) cone towering above the Neumarkt Galerie shopping center. The *Dropped Cone* sculpture was made to look like a giant ice cream cone that fell from the sky.

Hands On
Conrad the Cone

You can make and decorate a funny friend named Conrad the Cone. Ask an adult to help cut a cone net out of construction paper. Then assemble the cone and decorate it to make Conrad.

What You Need

 cone net cut from construction paper

 tape and glue

 scissors

 assorted decorations (felt, buttons, yarn, fake fur, feathers, googly eyes)

What You Do

1   Tape the straight sides of the sector together.

2   Tape the bottom of the sector to the circle base.

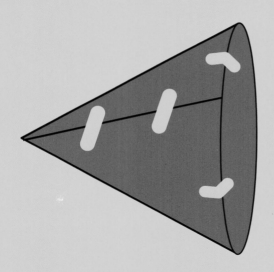

3   Glue decorations on the cone to make a funny face for Conrad.

Glossary

base (BAYSS)—a flat side that a 3-D shape stands on

depth (DEPTH)—how deep something is

height (HITE)—how tall something is

sector (SEK-tur)—a part of a circle made by drawing two straight lines from the center to different places on the outer edge

three-dimensional (THREE-duh-MEN-shun-uhl)—having length, width, and height; three-dimensional is often shortened to 3-D.

two-dimensional (TOO-duh-MEN-shun-uhl)—having height and width; flat; two-dimensional is often shortened to 2-D.

width (WIDTH)—how wide something is

Read More

Kompelien, Tracy. *3–D Shapes Are Like Green Grapes! Math Made Fun.* Edina, Minn.: Abdo, 2007.

Senisi, Ellen B. *A 3–D Birthday Party.* Rookie Read–about Math. New York: Children's Press, 2007.

Internet Sites

FactHound offers a safe, fun way to find Internet sites related to this book. All of the sites on FactHound have been researched by our staff.

Here's how:

1. Visit *www.facthound.com*
2. Choose your grade level.
3. Type in this book ID **1429600489** for age-appropriate sites. You may also browse subjects by clicking on letters, or by clicking on pictures and words.
4. Click on the **Fetch It** button.

FactHound will fetch the best sites for you!

Index

2-D shapes, 4

3-D shapes, 5, 6

bases, 6

castles, 13, 15

circles, 4, 6, 7

cone nets, 7

depth, 5

hats, 11, 26

height, 5

ice cream cones, 25, 26, 27

rhinoceroses, 22, 27

snails, 20, 27

width, 5